# SILT

## POEMS

# J P ROGERS

**[[*Chichen Itza* BOOKS]]**

ISBN: 978-1492840633

*For my son, who contributed to the making of some poems and inspired others.*

# CONTENTS

## LAKE

Hard as bone, this thing cracks the surface
in your lake of memory for an instant
and is gone; it is made of a different substance than you are.

What it takes when it slips away again is incalculable.
Arms cannot hold what lives in you alone.

We break apart in chunks as statues do,
new areas exposed to the pain of air and light.
The story is there if you need it:
an idea from the fog, a stranger to become, the ink of night
tattooed on your neck over time.

None of this was mandated, but leave it alone;
count each glacial breath and wait for delivery.
Read this now, if you will —
the sum of your life, etched on a single grain of rice.

## A REQUEST

Understand this, please: you are remembered — and always
will be — but for reasons slightly less precious than you might
hope (it's simply because you were there for some of my best
early disasters). Sure, existence is no carnival. Sure, it's
shameful to be living so far from safety, so roiled by the tongue
of faith. But this is what you taught me... I often have to rewind
it all to when good and bad were the same. That is when I am
most real, and I can leave this new kind of thinking alone and
see you like no other, locked in the soft jaws of the summer we
met, licked clean again by what could still be. But reality is a
persistent devil, and the reality is that I am now a deep
machine, and you are more like milk... I remember you, though.
I remember the note you left on my window: *blue saddle shoes
and cream soda* — which summed up your childhood.
Childhood is a dog that we forgot to untie when we left the
park — we tried to go back, but it was gone. All children
become gone, in one way or another. We don't ever get to
know what happens. Nearly every second, I could cry at the
jagged beauty of it.

## AUTONOMY

Advice from the margins is designed to please the giver. Don't
waver from your scent; run hotter, more touch-hungry.
Collapse is a real consequence but rarely happens.
Walk an accidental floor, notice nothing there
except a shadow like a face full of mouths
all now starving due to silence of
no one in particular, save the
one broken boy with
shut-off eyes
just like
you.

## EVERY GOOD BOY DOES FINE

### 1

Now he is small. He talks to spiders. I ache the way he aches —
an ashy blue pain we call Zeus. His skin speaks through such
trouble, but I cannot always hear it. I once wrote him a letter
that said, "Your hand is the ocean, mine is the sky." I planted it
under a tree in the yard for good measure. The birds
understood.

### 2

Now he is older, and the world is moving in. Everything has a
box where it belongs, but some of them are hidden for years. I
tell him not to be discouraged — there are ways around this. A
new space forms every hour. People will say, "Change your
name, or you will be plagued by opposites all your life."
Nobody listens. Nobody should.

### 3

Now he is away, like the rest. Time writes all the tiny books I
read. Keeping everyone cornered in my head is pointless; if I
free them, I might follow. Such is the house desire builds. There
are wolves living on the roof. Hope comes with wine in the
dark, but flows out again like the tide. No matter. At the end of
the day, I want the day to end. I speak to him always in our
prior language. He is fine. I am fine.

## THEY

They will always make it seem as if they know better than you do. When they tire of that, they cry and act hurt if it gains them something — forever lashing out from smaller places, trying to defend what they only presume. They suck the night in deeper, and leave you with just a sliver of moon. "Fine," you think, "Have Big Mind, swallow this tablet — it's seven days' worth of humility." Let it dissolve in your ear. Let your ear dissolve the dirt. This is the dirt they will bury you in. They will smile at you there, tucked under planet-skin, swimming in the red dirt like a backwards Jesus, *getting nowhere*. They're always smiling somewhere. You know where they are. You know where they are always — the sound of the ice clinking in their glasses may as well be a bell on a kitten's neck. They surround you, and they know nothing. But they will always make it seem as if they know everything you don't.

## AMNESTY

I often think of granting myself amnesty
wiping spent thoughts and scattering
the past; its wounds shed, sins absolved
(mine and the world's). Scrap it all
and live now on a new earth, poles reversed,
magnetic field flipped, forgetting
even how I came to be this smooth
new animal untouched by regret.
When it happens, my head will breathe
a pure moist silence to sweep away
those grinding days on dead necks
craned to spy on all hearts, and those nights
where in the slow hands of worry
I slept on dirty mounds that sang my name
and would wake, dazed, in the same salty skin
only to think again of granting myself amnesty.

## MONOLOGUE

Take it down a notch. We're aware of my limitations in this area. No one needs to see what's on offer here. Is this what you've come to expect? There's no telling who might be next to go, so watch your step. There are tigers on the prowl here — I've seen them. I don't want to go to bed yet, but I think I'm already asleep. There's too much pepper in this broth. There's too little warmth in this room. There's a pile of ash where some of my friends used to be. There is no time left for such nonsense. This isn't nonsense. It's not nonsense if you can grasp it. Understanding is the key to all doors. A skeleton key only opens crappy locks, I think. A master key opens them all. Master and skeleton. A blank is a key that hasn't been made yet. Yes, that's right. What was I looking for again? I'm serious, now, but no one is ready to accept that. Wait, what was that last thing? I really don't know why clocks continue moving when the time was just fine to begin with. I suppose each moment needs a name for purposes that are not visible yet. But clocks don't really move; just their hands do. What if clocks themselves moved, and you could tell the time by where in the room your clock was? Clocks and cars are practically the same. If you keep driving, you'll be somewhere else soon. Somewhere else is always a possibility, but not for me, since I am always here.

## WHAT I DID LAST WEEKEND

1. Woke up on a bed of rice at a restaurant where shame is the wine steward.
2. Initiated a small crisis that might someday come to be admired by many.
3. Passed several hours clinging to the fur of a childhood still in doubt.
4. Lifted a skirt with my eyes because it was in the way.
5. Carved thirteen sharp monsters straight from memory, then sent them away in a bus driven by murder.
6. Had some friends over, but the doors went missing again — they left through the window in the side of my mind.
7. Painted the ever-growing wall of amendments with red semen that can only be removed by eggs.
8. Accepted the past as a coal that will eventually burn out if I let it.
9. Launched a class-action suit against the vendors of neglect.
10. Made a pen from an owl feather and wrote my name on the list of people I will never meet.

## AT DAWN

Morning light is abusive. Certain kinds of brightness invite disaster, or at least showcase the possibility of it — an x-ray of existence that bares a growth you don't want to see. Dusk is preferable, when everything cools and gets off your back for a while. Dreams are useful, but too soft to build on. Each day rolls in the same way, soaking you with fresh thought. A cat prowls the yard at dawn. She knows that a certain kind of bird could be hers if she is correct in her movement. You can see this knowledge from your bedroom window. A cat and a bird are essentially the same. Things collide and break apart constantly, and all that is changed is our perception. You have always known this, yet today it is somehow a greater truth. Morning light forces you to realize there is no such thing as *nothing*. There never has been.

## STUYVESANT SQUARE

**I**

It all seems so long ago now but I am standing by a park in the
East Village with that late-afternoon, you're-at-your-own-
wake-but-it's-somehow-more-like-a-graduation sort of feeling,
fading light like giant spiders crawling through concrete
valleys, thinking of the fresh death in my life, and I remember a
day, ten years earlier still, sitting on a curb in front of my
sister's home, ready to leave the country and start over again
— and it is so hard to go anywhere ever and abandon the
locker of memory and all those beginnings (some not ended). I
am consumed at once by a particular strain of grief exiled for a
decade — a wandering hurt that returns to me because it fits
me and has nowhere else to go. It knocks me to the sidewalk;
my vision runs cast iron and bluestone. The gurgle of the
fountain in the park is the entire voice of beyond...

**II**

I rise from the ground with a sense that I am buried deep
inside the cold spectacle of New York, a minor figure in a
postcard of the collective reality. There is no one around —
such relief in the sheer miracle of no one walking on Second
Avenue. To the city, I am no more real than a guy in a movie
showing in an empty theater. I stare through the park fence at
a tree that could be my life: many-veined, awash in artificial

18

light, standing out ghoulish like the one tree dressed for Halloween among the normals. Taxis race by. They are senseless machines. They do nothing but rush, the clouds overhead rush, too, and the movie that is mine goes on for anyone who *could be watching*. But who is there to make a hero of me, to elevate my suffering? That is the terminus of this particular train. I have a place to go, so I button my coat and start going there.

## DREAM BOY

Dream Boy comes back into
your life and fucks it up
if even for just the moment you
rely on him to be someone new
this time, a hot coin to buy
some peace and ward off the anxiety
that pushes this idea of him
further from resolution.

Swallowing bright eggs oversalted
with spring promise
and pondering Dream Boy offers
nothing but a sour gut
and this hint that flits
about the corners of the room
"just out of reach" (he laughs inside you)
not able to be captured whole
or even just smashed.

## THE CALL

The dream is always the same, viewed through the prism of the backward: Standing at a payphone in a crowded bar in Brooklyn, early evening. The pulse of unheard music. The laughter of strangers. What's left of the sun reflects off a tall glass on a corner table, projecting a small circle of light on the wall near me. The circle is a perfect, empty presence — a signal from nowhere, open to interpretation...

I need to call a man on the other side of the country. Entering the string of numbers, each time my finger fails me and presses the wrong button. I have to start again. This happens over and over, and frustration takes hold. It occurs to me that the person I am calling is using their phone as a sort of poppet, pressing the buttons exactly as I am doing it here, deliberately warding off my attempt to reach them. I am being blocked, canceled out, and my fingers are reacting to this interference. I try again, get through five numbers, then miss on the sixth...

Hanging up, I look toward the bar where a young woman sits, waiting for me. Her face is not visible from this angle. She is wrapped in the same dying sunlight the glass projects. Someone shouts on the sidewalk outside. She turns toward me...

Suddenly realizing that all numbers are the same, and the phone itself is a trick designed to obscure this fact, I dial again without regard for correctness or sequence. The man on the other side of the country answers. Before I can say a word, he describes the circle of light on the wall next to me. "Perfect, empty."

## DRAMA

We watch because we cannot help it. Each day it unfolds right there in the front room of the house of time, with singular purpose — a deliberate show of affection for everything and its opposite. This is improvisation. There is no script or storyline to follow, no routine to fall back on. Just us and this blunt spectacle, with only the instrument of cognition to process it. The toolbox on the floor is filled with broken handles, headless things good for holding, but little else. The absence of structure is startling. The walls that used to keep things separate have been translated out of existence; we are now free to become our own children. Does this drama include its own justification? For those who notice such things, there are three books on the table. One is all covers, and the second has feathers where the pages should be. It is the third one that speaks as we look on. This is the narrator, spewing dust into our ears and eyes, but the message inside is clean: We watch because it is not over, and the tickets have already been paid for.

## NOWHERE

First thing is this: Are we still mammals?
Is there value in our connections,
the aluminum tendrils in skin
that ultimately trigger decay?

Age is a lion that shadows us all,
flashing a tooth to
insinuate grief — have you seen him?

In the years we have control,
why bind ourselves to this house?
Bacon and cigarettes and a pound
of glory, a life to be gained
from a damp sheet in
the third-floor bedroom — is this
what to hope for here?

The answers will be wrong, that's true,
but are the questions correct?
We'll accept that they are, so what is
the half-life of confidence, and which
flag of safety can you raise for me now?

There is a map to this place,

24

but everyone knows it's invisible;

do you know the way?

## GRAVITY

He always believed that gravity paid special attention to him.
Since childhood he had a notion that it lifted him slightly
sometimes, or gently moved him sideways — not always
pushing down. It simply had different ideas for him, he figured,
and in return, he felt he knew it more deeply than most. When
his head filled with trouble, he would call on gravity to drag it
away. This never worked out, but it did not shake his belief.
(Moments of need cannot be used to define universal forces,
and proof of this cohesive power was ubiquitous, after all.) If
he were ever truly overwhelmed, he was sure gravity would be
there to tug him back from the brink of the unknowable, to
soothe him with pure physicality. He appreciated that gravity
was a constant in his life, a sort of unseen parent, and no
matter what he could or could not achieve, it would be there,
embracing him and grounding him. The comfort and fairness
inherent in gravity as a companion was precious to him.
Because of their relationship, he was hopeful that when he
died, gravity would grant his final wish and not allow his body
to be planted in the earth, but instead fling him high into the
air with such velocity that he would explode into a million
grains of flesh and bone, which would then surrender to
gravity again and fall like sleet on those who would bury him.

## MIDNIGHT

Surprise yourself again — now waking in the hold of your ship of thought, course and speed unknown. West-by-north is a guess, but with no stars or horizon, just an idea tangled in degrees and knots. Your hull groans through the chop. Portholes at the waterline offer views of secrets too heavy to keep. Weight is the enemy of luck, and luck is the currency of the ocean. At exactly midnight, someone says, "This ship's engines run solely on regret." But there is no one else on board. From up on the weather deck, the sea reveals itself as a vast field of mirrors, each reflecting a grotesque marionette controlled by The Other. In the radio room, machines wake themselves and urgently telegraph: "This is not what you are looking for..." You draw a breath and hope the message is picked up somewhere. A huge fish with no eyes breaks the surface off the port bow, ending the tyranny of the moment. The sea-mirrors are shattered; *they cannot move with the ship.* The black wind whips your flag, offers faint praise for a job half-done.

## NAME

He has only one name left,
and it is deep blue.

Blue is the cushion of sleep,
a raft on which to lay
the sores each night.

Night is where a thousand
distant lamps broadcast
the lessons of solitude.

Solitude is written in the river
of the mind, gray and speckled
like an old dog.

Dog is what runs backward
in our own skin;
we look beneath this
and say, "Yes, it is he."

He has only one name left.

## THE SECRET

I'll offer you a hint:
Don't give up.
(That one was in language.)

Read the footprints of strangers.
Know exactly what you don't.
Use those sounds living
in your throat now
to feed the ears nearest you
(the best birds do this).

Keeping memory at bay,
there is enough time
to see all things done.

## SHE KNEW HALF

I

Rough weather always came from the West; she appeared on the horizon in the East. We rode bare, in the old style, until it was new again. Nothing until something. She came offering more than short answers. She grasped the value of remorse, in a forward-looking sense. She had worked it out on yellow paper and kept the figures in her purse (she was one to show her work). And we completely understood back then — dogs of a feather and all. She needed a little more length or slack to reach the failing heart of the matter, which will trigger alarms in the basement of paradise if pressed. As for me, I knew her as well as I could, often. She knew exactly half of all there was, plus one-quarter of what would be. Somehow in this process of becoming, we chose not to. All cannot be well until it all ends. This rocky wisdom will break teeth, so best to swallow it whole and forget whatever hasn't happened yet. I once found a map that would have led us to a logical conclusion, but she took me to a place with no air instead. I stayed for two-and-a-half years, thinking sideways, eating only sound. The day I left, I was informed by the trees lining the road that she never existed. *If only you had seen this coming*, they whispered.

## II

When I found him, he was braced for impact. He needed to know if nothing and something were still on speaking terms. The short answer is too long to get into here, but a pound of regret will outlast a pound of promise. (Yes, it's sad.) Given so many choices, we are bound to become something we don't choose in the end. By the time I left, I had him convinced I was never there. I locked the door and reimagined the key as a bright green bird, then chased it off into a cloud. And that was that... *With a hundred eyes, he could not have seen this coming.*

## HOPE

Sometimes when I am most haunted by the ghosts of my own making, I think of the day of the engagement party in New York — not of the party itself, but of you... Unpack it slowly, so as not to miss anything: A Saturday in May, early afternoon. I come to your apartment alone. You are standing by the bed washed in sun as I empty my bag. You want to wear my shirt because you like the shade of green. You strip off what you have on, no ceremony — an unconscious act that explodes the room and reclaims just enough of the city to host a sliver of gold days, when breasts were as common as beer cans yet prized like alluring new friends. You flash a cool grin as you slip into the green shirt. Something pulses in your eyes. Almost to yourself, you say "Pardon my tits," with a whispered laugh that dissolves immediately into pure light. You look up at me, a lean-meat foal ready to break out of that place and run off with every last prize — offered or not.

## SEPTEMBER NIGHT, RAIN

Summer left today, and tonight a hard rain.
My son sleeps in the crook of my arm,
lips slightly parted, as breath rolls
with the ease of ocean waves.

Later, when the storm has moved on
I visit my favorite tree.
Cloud veils rise on a tide of stars
and present the cool face of autumn.

Night tastes sweet among pines, but I do not linger.
The swollen moon hurries me along
with an admonition: *Days are growing short.*

## AWAKE

I have just now awakened
to find I am trapped in this place
with the three things
that bother me most —
past, present and future.

There is no exit, save for a door
that is too busy screaming
to be a door.

A song made entirely of silence
plays far away, in the land
my voice comes from.

If I can hear it, so can you.

## NOT YET

I can't forget. Not with crumbs of that failure still stuck in my whiskers. Do you have any idea? It's like hot spaghetti on a white shirt — you can wipe it off, but it stays with you — it's grease, oil. It's a stain. You've heard of a stain, yes? Well, it's more than a word, than a sound you can make with your mouth. It's something objective that won't go away, something that can come to define you if you let it. Will you accept being stained? No. Just need to regroup, outrun the echoes of last winter that still try to undermine reality. These aftershocks keep coming, albeit at ever-decreasing frequency. Scary when they come, though. Failure amid the echoes cannot be considered — not yet anyway. It's still early by some measures. Have to root through all these closets and see what's left, what I can use to build better defenses, stave off the decline of the self in the eyes of the other, or the eyes of the self, or the new eyes of history that are being formed in every socket as we speak. As we speak, or as we don't speak. Whether we speak or not, things will happen just the same. Noise has no intrinsic value, or it would go by a different name. And you can call your noise anything you like — groundbreaking, critical. Regardless, if there really is a shepherd in charge of us all, he will recognize your noise no matter what. You can be identified by noise and stain as easily as by fingerprint. Change your shirt, give the old one a new name, too, and the echoes still find you, because

35

they are yours. If you made the sound, you own the echoes. It's an intractable relationship. Even so, I will handle this. I'll tend the wound, because it's the one I know. I'm onto something here; I'm close. Things get better often. But if time heals all wounds, why is it in such short supply? The hospitals and churches and factories should be making it for us. It may well be late in the game, but there's still a lot to play for. Are you ready to declare victory? Are you ready to admit defeat? Just pick a card and get it over with?

## STUMBLE

Shadows predict when we stumble into the last ravine and find
messages were leaking from cracks in the earth all along.
When we see that responsibility is an illusion. And so forth.

Stones know how we struggle when the façade gives way
and every change around here becomes semi-permanent.
If changes read like notes from your better half on the fridge
then they might be. No matter what the words, they will say:
*Without all the dying, life loses two-thirds of its value...*

My guess: We'll eat just enough shit
to fertilize a fresh understanding,
an ounce or two of clarity to waste
on those shiny birds we love best,
with proud accusations that getting old
is what we live for, that this intercourse
with things is the wrong way home,
that this new weather has no edges,
that there's nothing on the other side of now.

## WHEN HE AWOKE

with his finger in the socket of wisdom
he feared all answers, but stayed long enough
to indemnify himself from amnesia
then outran the devil all the way south
stopping just once to play tag with young rabbits
(normally disguised by impersonating plants
but now unafraid in plain sight)
while at home in a vacuum his own true babies
had grown too big to be ignored
and moved on hand-in-hand
like a slow secret train.

## THE BEDROOM LESSON

Upstairs alone, late-night reading. The house generating soft noises, the yard listening. All thought detached, gone into a thin yellow book for a while, then suddenly jolted back into *now* by the notion that others perceive and accept some of the same things you do (a common external reality amid the sprawling, broken circus of all this). We hold fast to colors, numbers and such — anything we can all agree on. And words. They collect in dark corners, waiting to be assembled into something more permanent. Original ideas or recipes for quiet. Suspension of belief, nonattachment, mindfulness — all scams. God is a simple instrument, a hedge against widespread deflation. (Haven't even met him; just happen to live in his old place.) Keep your distance close always, ready to spool out as needed. Who wants to be involved in this grand trick anyway, where everything does nothing but change and disappear? The water glass on the table fills with dust. A dying cricket chirps by the door in the basement.

## THE BEAR

"Just shut the fuck up forever," she said, and those words rang in my ears for nearly three weeks until the Great Bear of Internal Resistance came back from vacation and ate everything in sight, including what she said, what I said, and any conversational residue still around. I found myself back at the beginning of the end, with no end in sight, but with an outside chance to rewrite the backstory to the world's headache. I declined the opportunity. Instead I interviewed for a series of lesser positions in my own life, but did not receive any concrete offers. Dejected, I considered not being born at all, but my mother wouldn't hear of it. This is always the way it happens for guys like me when mouths get opened.

## I DREAMED YOU WERE A FAT, GOLD SNAKE

Last night in a moment of concern
I had you in my arms
when we were in love
you told me things I had not heard
in my life there are just enough
grinning saints to float above me
always when I die in dreams
I think of nothing except
you cannot kill me, ever.

## YOU & ME

### *YOU*

The day you married Mr. Holy, I brought flowers and kerosene — an attempt to make things right. The fires I could not set fueled a void we understood. We shared it with friends like a favorite record: just skeletons humming a birthday tune. For now, it's all the same, and our history is a thin film on cold soup. (There is no point in revisiting anything.) But of course the story cannot end there... Three years, and this: in a field north of the interstate, you crawl into a pile of fresh grievances and send us all a message about your bleeding hands and something to do with self-reliance that no one understands — just a rustling in the weeds. The rest of it will never be told. This is the nature of the void.

### *ME*

The ride is new and tastes like blood. The differences here are staggering. I awoke in a head filled with dust and a life reassembled while I was gone. Whoever orchestrated all this did a decent job, but there are things I might have done differently. And what if I could have simply *been* for a while — to see what existence itself had to say? Enough of that. At least the heart and stomach match. I am ready for the rest of it. I can do little wrong, nor much right. At the end of the day, it is none of my business what I believe. And, yes, death is sometimes all that keeps me alive — but it's a force stronger than anything you can imagine. This, too, is the nature of the void.

## THE TWO

If I can exist, so should you;
no one could deny such a thing.

From this point on we wait
for a strange current to carry us
toward the understanding that there
are only two elements:
Seen and Unseen.

For three weeks now
the walls in the room we shared
have been hanging their own pictures —
unused tools, an invisible ladder
a pair of empty chairs.

The quiet here
moves backward
toward the ceiling
and eventually collects
in a glass bowl by the door.
We can do little but look
as we pass by
in common awe
of all this and nothing.

## PRIZE

It arrived as a prize in a cereal box — something rigid in a
fistful of damp. It was extracted from a place it didn't belong,
where it was estranged from everything around it. Once
removed, it shone with the light of a true *thing*. I have only one
question: Where did it come from? Was it made by elves with
our well-being in mind? By workers in a mill that refines ideas?
By giant women who are 98% sex and 2% milk fat? Was it sent
electronically by common angels via a dedicated cable, one
perhaps reserved specifically for mild confusion? Did it emerge
from a dream, like the one where every friend I've ever had
(and one stranger) were asleep in a cabin by a laughing river?
Is this prize a down-payment on replacement dreams?
Collateral against debts accrued? Is this the prize we get when
all avenues have been explored? When the lights go out and the
moon is our only guide? Do we all get the same thing in
different boxes? I'll admit this may seem like more than the
one question I initially claimed to have — or are these just
variations of the same one? What is a question, and where does
it begin and end? I suppose it ends when we attempt an
answer, so here is mine: It came as a prize in a box, which is
normal enough. I have no intention of giving it up. The rest of
the answer is still being formulated, and will be shaped by
further questions that have yet to present themselves. But for
now I have the detail of the box, which, when taken apart and

laid flat, can be used as a map. I am pretty sure this is one detail the devil cannot find his way into — not even my devil. I am pretty sure this prize signifies something primal. I am pretty sure we figure it all out, just in time to exit this place with a shit-eating grin.

## THE JOURNEY

The fourth day out we
saw The Demon;
He was a woman, red
wig and a harelip,
told us all about
life underground and said
Jesus was a fag.

That night He
showed us his sores
took away the atmosphere
and was gone —
we heard Him rot.

Fifteen days since then
and we still haven't made it.
Chief says two more days
tops, so we push on
and think only of mother
but nothing's happened since
the fourth day out.

At night I wonder:
What did He mean by that wig?

## FOUR HUTS

There are four huts in my mind
each with an element of safety
and an equal element of fear.
The days are spent crawling
from one to the other
to see which lamp is burning
brighter in the window
for the time being.

On the wall of each hut
hangs a mirror made of steel
framed by memory and polished
with blood and saliva.

These mirrors reflect only
what they know to be false
and keep the rest trapped inside.
This is the way they build
the power needed to one day
break free of frames and burn
all four huts to the ground.

Like it or not, since childhood
I have known it must be that way.

## THE PLAN

Exploding heads were everywhere, bits of skull and gray matter filling the sky and pelting the frozen ground. (*This is an actual brainstorm*, he thought, which struck him as humorous.) He knew his own head would be fine, since he had certain power the others did not. The way he saw it, they practically let this happen — maybe even wanted it to. As for him, he planned on waiting the whole thing out and then assuming a life he had carefully stolen from another man's dream one night last winter. He had been sneaking into strangers' bedrooms and monitoring their dreams for years, looking for something that was rich in flesh and comfort, and which had every indication of being impervious to bad fortune. Since he stole it, it had been wrapped in a soft cloth at the bottom of his sock drawer, where no one would reasonably expect to find it. As soon as all this tumult subsided, he would pull it out, fully recharge it and dive right in. This was going to be so good, and maybe it would last forever. Meanwhile, all those around him made slow, troubled noises as they waited for their turn to come.

## THE TRICK

We woke up in the room of refusal for the last time. The old cock outside the window declined to crow, but was willing to speak: It was a hard morning. He begged us to spill the horn of plenty and cut the telephone line. This was all a trick. Sometimes the phone is called 'the horn' — or at least it used to be. The cock knew this, but only halfway. He spit the idea of a stone onto the floor where we stood, and was gone. Everything went with him. To this day, when we think about the nothings we have, and the nothings we can't, we look back at that morning as the beginning. It really was.

## BURN

In a slow-burning field
a clock argues with itself
just before dawn
and cannot seem to win.
Coils and springs are tangled
in veins of blue ice.

At either end of the field
a chalk-white face stares
into a fractured mirror
looking for something
other than reflection.

The truth left on scorched earth
has the substance of moonlight;
it's the same message as ever —
too early to be your own teacher,
too late to make this chance count.

## THE ALLEGORY OF THE MISSING DAY

And so it was that a certain day went missing from the calendar on the big wall, but the day it was due to be found was the same one. Those closest to the wall feared great panic or worse — the plague of nothing, sinkholes in memory, a ferocious storm of zeros. A team of experts was assembled, and they worked on the problem around the clock (which, thankfully, cared nothing for dates). This effort continued right up until the eve of the missing day, when it was judged that the day in question hadn't existed in the first place. This was the easiest way forward, they assured us. There were no questions asked.

## THE ANECDOTE OF THE BOTTLE

"I'm burying these sentences in a bottle right here," she said, "so someone can dig them up and have them for a while." The bottle was bare, label long gone, such that all language involved in this transaction would be hers.

That is what she hoped for — to change one patch of ground with a few ideas that leaked from a well of deep feeling within her, and thus make the earth there a grave for her mood exactly as it existed that one January afternoon when she found no warmth in her pockets, only the tiny yet perfectly formed bricks of truth she carried to one day build a fitting tribute to all she hoped to destroy.

## YOUR STRANGER

Begin with a number no one uses — the square root of purple.
Add to it the facts that all life is criminal, and there is only so
much closet space. I am not allowed to have your thoughts, but
can admire the view from them anytime.

A toast to you, then: Placenta pills and cocktails all around.

Those who dwell in stone houses learn to throw glass instead.
You will come to love this place if you stay. You will say "Eat
my philosophy" to all who enter... Well, you should know that I
am Your Stranger.

I am around every day. I am in your bedroom right now. Maybe
I'm the horse that sings you to sleep. Or a charismatic ape.
Maybe I'm the bear that will replace you...

Look: You can see my education reflected in the mirror in this
miniature photograph. Look more carefully: I am cold and full
of knives. I have pictures of your music. I watched you turn
faith into a noisy screwdriver. Are we all screws now?

One last thing, before I move on: Be wary of facts that crave
motion. You can flush these words away, but they will ruin you
just the same. *It's already done.*

## TWILIGHT

Apologies to all
that the light in my head
has been out for a while.
During this time giraffes
stalked me in the darkness
with teeth that were not theirs.
They were looking for a radio
broadcasting news of water and trees,
yet they heard nothing
but the wind delivering old truths:
Not everyone is special.
There is only so many nights.
This life has no name.

## PROPOSALS

### I

Intelligent new people
buy affordable luxuries —
have the days under your control
no matter where you are.
Become a prolific man.
Change your life today.

### II

You will sleep hard tonight when
your profile is locked in
response to a complaint
received by the Administration.

### III

You need to take these pills
to experience nirvana.
Xanax? Percocet? Valium?
Natural and safe enhancing
all for your carnal plethora.

### IV

Get better in making it with her.
Solutions for ero-exploits and

protection against bed weakness
will let you accomplish fantasies
get convexity on jeans
realize amorous scenarios
and feel the scent of love again.
Some extra vigor with ease;
make your volcano
erupt more lava.


**V**

Russian queens are waiting.
I, sexual Russian blonde,
want to see, come closer.
Do you want me again?
A dream to live abroad —
my name is Mary —
can we get started? There are
eleven new ladies here; come in to me.
You are my good, my handsome,
write me, I'm waiting!
I am your Russian pussy —
you remember my nickname?

## THE ANSWER

Erase the route that runs through here and outlines our heat in
blue pencil. Cancel the whole map, in fact. Redraw the wind so
it propels only sunk boats. Then give it a face and call out each
compass point it plays against — the first is as good as the last,
so one big name should do. The compass itself will expose
North but cannot say what's there, even if you beg. Could be
paradise or a toothache. Could be a granite figure of a woman.
A woman is a compass, too, with true breath in the dark and all
those fingers. Someone said you can lead a woman to hunger
but cannot make her stay. Someone said too much. I didn't hear
what was asked, but I know the response everyone's looking
for. Why is it always the worst questions that answer
themselves? That's what I thought right before I stopped.

## THAT'S WHY WE COME

It hails from everywhere that is nowhere and is notoriously
giant, so by all means, call it what you wish to make it smaller:

1. a whisper of ice
2. baby's silver tongue
3. recent stones in seawater

We don't usually do this... But for you it's all right. That's why
we come here, to dress you up and down, leave you asleep on
the ceiling slightly closer to various heavens. So far, so good.
We come here with analogues for your words. The language is
broken, so we don't use it anymore. You can see what this
means, can't you? Just like all your favorite predictions are
made of air, all the best nowheres live right here. It's difficult to
recall what hasn't been learned yet, but we are working on it.
For now, let this be a lesson, or a cure for thought.

## NOTES ON HEAVEN

Heaven does not exist.

Heaven quite possibly does exist.

Heaven is located on a map I keep in the back pocket of my desire.

Heaven can be found anywhere, without a map, even in Kansas.

Heaven is a really big deal.

Heaven is located between a woman's thighs, and has many different hairstyles, but you will recognize it.

Heaven has blue eyes and black hair, always.

Heaven is vast field of nipples.

Heaven is an idea whose time has come.

Heaven is where, when you need to go there, they don't have to let you in.

Heaven is a currency used by gamblers and thieves.

Heaven is a drug, in the same family as codeine.

Heaven is a car filled with dead birds.

Heaven is where mean people have no tongues.

Heaven can be seen directly through a conduit located in the left eye of a freshly killed deer on the side of the highway.

Heaven is two cats cleaning each other, yet still fighting.

Heaven is a turtle with shiny metal wheels.

Heaven has been discovered, in minute amounts, in panda dung.

Heaven is where snakes have hips.

Heaven implies the freedom to fuck up your own life.

Heaven is a 97-mph fastball aimed straight at your skull.

Heaven is a radio that broadcasts deafening pauses.

Heaven is a parade of five-year-olds in Halloween masks.

Heaven is a parade of 85-year-olds whose faces have become masks.

Heaven is a 44-year-old woman with Down Syndrome who tickles your nose and smiles, but does not speak.

Heaven is a hat we all wear on occasion that covers our eyes and ears.

Heaven, like Pluto, will soon be demoted to a minor planet.

Heaven moves each September, but won't file a change-of-address form.

Heaven has lost roughly 27% of its value in the last year.

Heaven is a dominatrix who loves kicking your ass in front of the neighbors.

Heaven is a monster truck driven by a bad-tempered toddler.

Heaven is a camera that captures our every action so we can feel awful about it later.

Heaven is made entirely of Lincoln Logs soaked in gasoline.

Heaven tastes something like an ice cube.

Heaven smells like grass and smoked fish.

Heaven is a song with no notes, only breaks and fills.

Heaven is a clock without hands.

Heaven is a plant that shuns water and light, but thrives on good conversation.

Heaven is a balloon filled with cancer.

Heaven is where important messages are delivered by spiders.

Heaven is an ejaculation of color and sound that means nothing, but looks impressive.

Heaven is policed by 18 happy women and one surly robot.

Heaven is a hot dog stand at the end of the road by an empty beach.

Heaven is a smiling rat.

Heaven comes in tiny plastic bags.

Heaven can sometimes be reached only by canoe.

Heaven requires all who enter to have no skin.

Heaven is where they filmed 'Night of the Living Dead.'

Heaven is a glacier, conceived by all sentient beings, that melts only when we are thirsty.

Heaven sends black helicopters to rescue common saints dying on the streets of our cities.

Heaven is best served at room temperature, in digestible portions.

Heaven is a simple machine that manufactures patience.

Heaven is an anthill populated only by queens, where nothing ever gets done.

Heaven is where everyone exists always, whether we like it or not.

Heaven is a house on a bluff overlooking a river of poison.

Heaven will rip you to pieces if you're not tough enough.

Heaven is no match for a quiet mind.

## TALL

This might be the tallest I've ever been, but it depends on which plane you're looking from. I'm getting close to outgrowing the suit of problems that regret made for me. (The most uncomfortable fabrics are often those we cannot see.) Most things get closer every day. And the noise. I've asked my son to use his three-inch voice — framed in the widest margin for error he has — when questioning me. At least until I get used to all this size. When he was very young and had no size to speak of, he said: *Being dead is not good for the body.* His logic was sound. The fact that he was thinking about death at all I simply took as further evidence that sometimes our life is the unluckiest place on earth.

## ELEGY

Begin with the end: *You drown in sand* at the edge of the sea,
knowing it's the same as anything new — get it done, and
you're through to the next round. As sunlight bottoms out,
recall the line of men and women dangled by our gods in the
dimly painted space around life. Accept a furious truth to take
with you: All is exactly how it is, and nothing is at all how it
was. (It likely never was.) At the very end, rescue should arrive
atop a female voice through a slurry of humming bones — too
late.

\*\*\*

Begin with the middle: To sit atop these flames, laughing,
implies more than one master. We shed the cloak of proximity
to chase sudden beauties, but in which mirror does one find his
original face? Our universe is always leaving, but if we rebuild
the eye in the clouds, we'll see each other again — without
seeing a thing. Once you watched yourself die, only to be
reborn in blue fire. So you kept dying a little. This is all just
slow-moving violence.

\*\*\*

Begin with the beginning: The grandfather of violence is a blow to the base of the skull that radiates from the zero spot, rings of blindness soaking city blocks, senses canceled, whole animals failing. Humans searching for a river in which to sink their fear. You learn to ignore fear early on. It goes wherever it wants anyway, sustained by hope, outpacing all and nothing — one and the same. You knew from birth that all accounts would be settled before the imagination decays. The grandson of violence is a hot blast to the temple that brings clarity, forces you to know you are someone real. Not just a tiny snake inside of a head, safely scanning confusion.

***

Begin with nothing: Ideas are good at holding ground, and most will do for quick shelter if needed. Your demise was preordained by cowgirls with white-cake thighs calving the truth at every angle. Heaven isn't here right now. In the sand at the edge of the sea, shells and driftwood pulse with amnesia as a vast factory of pain shuts down. The last of the wind shares a secret: *You will not solve time.* A moon pulls itself up drowsy ladders, and quiet gathers like a flock of gulls.

## THE FISHERMAN

The broken fisherman casts his doubt in multiple directions,
ensuring surface tension is evenly swallowed. It's hard to
watch for too long. He thinks of fish as geniuses because they
don't bother with anything behind them. They know this, but
say little — take his bait and go. The fish gave birth to the
fisherman, and would be content to leave it at that. You and I
can learn from this. In the lives we invent by accident each day,
a fish is a highway sign written in movement. It's not easy to
read at our rate of travel, so we check the atlas to be sure. It
indicates that all roads paved with intentions head south
eventually, so I'll just meet you there.

## WHAT REALLY HAPPENED

Just then I was able to will myself off the ground with intense concentration and constriction of the muscles in my torso, and float freely, as high as I liked — yet at the same time, I realized I could always do this. I was hovering right above the powerful smelting machine that breaks us down and reassembles us as our fathers when a very tall woman began wrapping the clouds in blankets. They were woolen and brightly colored, but looked abrasive. I watched for a while before a sense of loss stabbed me in the neck. I fell to the ground. The tall woman was gone. It was then I realized she had only come to distract me while someone else reached into my pocket and snatched the oldest words I owned. I felt terrible because they were from my mother, and I considered them irreplaceable. Suddenly my mother was there. She looked me square in the eye and said, "I never did like you." Her voice was like a church organ, but I could understand. *My own mother*. It was shocking, but not as shocking as the blankets, and how tall that woman was. Soon it was as if the stolen words hadn't existed anyway. All of the letters in all of those words became silent one by one, and night fell right on time.

## WINTER

On the coldest nights, he seeks out signs of intimacy among local machines — drive shafts and belts, hoses greased and knowingly entwined. Just like the cluster of hooded snakes living on the ceiling above his bed. Intimacy always seems hidden in the walls, or obscured by dirty sound. So many places to be lost. At home, in a sack of holy things, he keeps a thin red stone plucked from a grave he knows. It was intended as a key to unlock his space in the new atmosphere, or a dagger for ending his long-standing feud with the sky. On the most quiet nights, spitting promises like seeds into the air, it all takes much longer than expected... The scene stays the same: Moonlight sprayed on icy yards, a broken back and promise, a heart in a jar — this is all there is to work with. It's too little to reverse the metal tongues of winter now. Across a field, cell towers blink as scores of invisible messages take flight.

## FORGIVENESS

1. Go ahead: Slip off the birth-jacket as the haunted brain suggests.

2. Understand: Ghost bones are not fit to carry muscle. They just erode like stars at dawn.

3. Think: Decades spent amid the din of echoes can boil down to a single idea.

4. React: Stanch the worry with wads of kindness and remember all those futures.

5. Believe it: There are some who love living so much they cannot bear to do it so poorly.

6. Absorb: On a table by the door lie crumbs of thought to digest as night comes.

7. Forgive: Potential is the last thing to go; it exits through the eyes. The hands of the clock offer thin applause.

## TIME

If I hold on a minute too long, I can't sense it anymore — time, I
mean, cast as a net for gathering everything else's name.
Mistakes in judgment are likely to occur as the blizzard of data
that feeds us changes and is changed — silk to liquid and back.
What's this called again? A condition or set of symptoms that
can be identified and pressed into the one true shape of matter,
something like a clock embryo in a shot glass. What I mean to
think — what we all do, really — is that it's too hot inside this
ongoing embrace, and time will stop at nothing to make us half
again.

## PREDICTION

The sound is that of all numbers screaming at once, yet nobody hears it — too busy sitting around the old table making ideas. It will come again, but if still unheard, it moves on with the general current, borne back into its own history. This is the way it happens. Those at the table groom each other's apathy like cats. They are all sisters, even the men. But in the end, their collective purpose swells and ruptures into dozens of unbearable memories that reduce them to tears. Eventually someone will set the table on fire out of boredom metastasized for decades. Each one will rise and shout how they alone were correct in foreseeing this. I swear, this is the way it will be.

## CIRCLE

After decades the forgotten directions from childhood circle
home again. And of course you know them. It used to be that
lost causes stayed lost, but in light of new evidence surfaced on
the shoulders of children, you are now allowed to wait again —
to ring the bell and hope that earlier versions of yourself will
arrive. This could take a while, but you will eventually expect
what is learned. Have faith in the investment vehicle, where
growing old is the goal. Someday you will have your share of
the proceeds.

# HER DREAM

She would not ever stray from her belief that she could one day do the impossible, and that this would set her free. When her worst thoughts felt drawn too closely around her, she would attempt feats of liberation, which she would only describe as *playing with never*. She invariably failed, but did feel that each attempt made her stronger. Ultimately she concluded that freedom must exist outside the cloak of proximity, something like a boat all but lost on the horizon, seen from a beach. Something like a dream. And there were always the gorillas for that. Each night she would see roller derby in her sleep — with gorillas in glass tubes circling the ocean floor. Each one would take a turn skating to the front of the pack and then fade gently back, as the others slapped him and sang jingles from TV ads. When a gorilla made it to the front, he would say, *You can have the mountains; I'll take the seas.* She was more than OK with this proposal, because she loved the mountains, and she grew fond of the gorillas, too. She hoped that one night as she slept she could answer the gorillas, and spent several weeks working out what this answer would be. She finally settled on *suddenly, beautiful* because she thought the gorillas would understand. One night she managed to get these words out. The gorillas were stunned and broke from their normal behavior. They stopped skating and slapping and singing. The most sweet and gentle-looking gorilla of them all — in fact he had been her favorite for months — quietly stepped out of his glass tube and moved toward her. She smiled. The gorilla smiled back and said, *You're alive, you fuck, so just deal with it.* She awoke at that moment and did not see the gorillas again. She felt very alone for a while.

## PERFECT

Real desire began to consume him the very moment he
stopped trying to figure out how to make her perfect. He had
always reworked what she was, who she was, in his head,
adding only the small things here and there that he required to
make her the perfect mate. This was not a wholesale
redesigning of what she was, but merely tweaking,
troubleshooting her overall being — physical, emotional,
intellectual — and actually changing as little as possible. This
became the thing with him: seeing how few changes were
necessary to make her perfect, as a chess master surveys a
board and knows how many moves are necessary to reach the
desired outcome. Of course her current distance from
perfection would fluctuate based on many factors, moods and
physical variables, where some days she was excellent to him
and required few improvements, and other days she needed
real work. And sometimes he would allow himself only three
changes to her, as if granted wishes by a genie, and he would
weigh all the possibilities and figure out which ones were the
most critical.

Then one day when she was searching for something in the
closet, she opened his old brown bag, which she had not ever
touched. Inside, she found several open wounds, three big
mistakes, two sore spots and several nights before they met

that he wished had gone very differently. When he came home that evening, she emptied the contents of the bag on the bed, without a word. Then, after a few seconds, she strode out of the room, head held high, with a rigid, confident posture he had never quite seen before. Even from behind, he could see her smiling from the way her ears inched back. And that was it. From right then, he knew her, understood her, and he was overcome with the hunger.

## BLOODLETTING

It's brutal to think of them awash in the eternal ruining pulse of what we try so hard to mute. They used to be here always drawing us out like hot blood through gauze, and now stained by this absence we rise each day and eat our own thoughts — the bitter plants that grow inside. If we had the courage, we would scorch these fields and let them lie fallow until they stopped being dead just once.

## THE LOST HOUR

I only remember this: we were near the water, and in the twilight a troubled song escaped from the radio, as we begged for clarity at the lost hour. Just then the sky ran away for good. Stars dissolved into crystals of ash behind our eyes and were gone as if exhaled. I only remember this.

## VACANCY

The house of blindness is shut down for night. Rusted plants by the stoop point to a broken lake of sky. There is no safety *in things* at this late hour — steel animals use their own language in the dark. Sounds much like everything else, but you recognize it. The commonality of existence is airtight, and all houses are blood relatives. A house itself will only speak up to say: *Every one of us has been changed*, and *It's hard to believe what cannot be not heard*. When people go, their empty places become rigid and feral. The lack of material to work with is eventually alarming. You learn to give in... No soul in the attic here. No thunder in this rain.

## THE STORY INSIDE

### 1

He checks the listening voice
out from her place for help.
Just looking dumb for nothing
can be a job or something.
Stay up in his mouth and sit through it.
She has nothing over at the voice's place.
Everyone is your word for once.
Promises you know she wanted,
but maybe it's beneath her to try.
Hear the house with your hours.
Despite the bedroom with all the morning,
she remains where the listening voice came.
He might well be good or bad.
He has no answer but nothing.
Sometimes they cannot even thank hope.

### 2

Please, God will get his own door
drilled into the little mountain.
No need to think there.
Still he opens her mouth to leave.
We should borrow the door you two are closing.
Reach for something like a best friend.

Mouth pauses to follow the night,

hand in their way, and you just passing through.

Stop the smile of her gaze.

Folding her voice, she calls me alone.

Stop all the horses to take care.


**3**

Things in this forest look back.

He replies behind her.

Please make camp in my head.

She shakes him to loosen hard days.

Meals come out their eyes upon seeing.

Maybe you want it down in the face.

Maybe they say to make sure.

Maybe she grins her ear.

Maybe your back says something of another.

You must hear this to be done.

The table always makes its way around.


**4**

Black for what she sees to watch.

She must not have one to quiet her hands.

Would it be hers to run away?

She kisses him when things become.

There is warmth in 'maybe you'll stay.'

Black for what she moves away.

Deep sigh and speak of women.

Tears come with such things.

Sure, but she sees history now.

He only remembers the other side.

People are going for trouble;

wish we had gotten up for some.

Black for what she consumes again.

## 5

He changes the house

where she is the living room.

What he pulls, it means to calm.

She gives the end of course.

Funeral kitchen so much better.

God is your couch. Long enough.

She asked the apartment to speak.

It all felt like girls.

Maybe we can always try to talk.

Small words had marked his face.

He could hear the blanket.

Here until now they were doing okay.

Homegrown weeds. Homegrown rocks.

Turning to enjoy the luck, she got married.

Since then just tall squirrels.

## 6

Men will return to get lost
as they worry their way to reckoning.
People in her head; opening every word.
Need this weight and watch it, too.
That just about closed the book on
anything but right here.
Stay with each word of things.
She is coming to remember that,
so you best hide it right now.
She smiles as though the sunrise,
while the night keeps her family.
It's good to get along with such things.
She has less in her mouth than
words going back against the good.
They are ready for they.

## 7

Her own arm says nothing more.
Looking at the night, she feels good
remembering where her arms eat.
Even before we saw the spiders
she was losing our people.
She wonders if old enough is enough
because it reminds her of long things.
Leaning forward on closed eyes,

she looks hard at last night.
But instead she wants color.
Might have to use the white
without any cause to use the white.

**8**

When she catches his age
she knows where it was not.
She returns his voice to the table,
looks down in his pocket
where the women had been,
takes the whole scene with her.
She will lean back in years now.
Today is not even a real thing.
Biting her lips together, promises die.
Nothing is much like the talking.
Now happens all the time.
Which reminds us the abandoned house
still has our lives nailed to the door.

## BECAUSE I AM TRYING TO SOLVE MY PROBLEMS WITH LOVE

1. I will grab a fresh eraser; we all know me too well. I can become something else tomorrow. Perhaps a chicken or a dog — nothing too exhausting.

2. Threats are multiplying all the time. Our friends live in mortal fear they are going to be reupholstered. They know the exact date.

3. There are turtles that can approximate love for decades. Such things offer hope that we can overcome our lives. Love, as a tool, has so many opposites, but I'm keeping track of them... Will you help?

4. The mind and tongue form a deceptively simple machine: noise goes in; misunderstanding comes out. Or vice versa.

5. The day it was announced that hope was an incurable condition, we began waiting for instructions on how to proceed. Nothing has come yet. I check the mailbox every morning.

## COWGIRLS

All the cowgirls in all the dreams you can remember are
exactly the same — one eye missing, a broken canine and false
mouths drawn on. Skin so thin you can see the wasps
underneath. If given half a chance, these women would smash
your heart in the face with a shovel.

You keep certain truths among the sundries in your nightstand,
just in case:

- → Every life has side-effects.
- → No one else can give birth to you.
- → Your house is rebuilding itself.
- → There is an ocean with your name on it.

Each morning you vow that when you are a ghost, you will
haunt every last one of them. You will creep into their dreams
and plant ruin — yet not ever stay long enough to regret a
single red seed.

## LESSONS

### I

You are in the shop; a woman is standing near you. She turns slowly, leans, then falls over like a short, thick tree. Hits the floor hard, all belly and elbow and *ooof.* You rush to her, reach for her arm, ask if she is OK. Her face and eyes are a riot of confusion, yet she refuses help. You let go. She rights herself, first on all fours, then regains her feet. She reaches to gather her things. Eventually she steadies herself and limps through a door held for her. And it hits you: This is a brittle thing we have here, and love might be all that stands between us and the void... ever. You head out into the winter sun. To the left, the fallen woman is making her way along the sidewalk. To the right, a young couple is holding each other as they kiss — her hands are tucked inside his coat for warmth. For just a second, you are stuck. There is nowhere to go.

### II

You are sitting on the front step drinking the night air, and feel someone watching you. Doesn't make sense until you see that just a few feet away is a rabbit — nothing but deep black eyes. Neither of you moves for a minute, each afraid for different reasons. You try hard to be still. Rabbit seems very much like a girl you love, but you are not sure such things are possible. Eventually, she angles up on surprising legs and is off in an instant. You hear the vanishing. Look up and realize the night sky is actually the ocean, with sandbar clouds and currents of blue ink. You stand and see that your shadow is a strange giant swaying in the porch light — huge head and shoulders. He is not you, yet he leaves when you leave.

## THE TRUTH ABOUT NOW

- ❖ *Now* is a hot lie hidden in the germ of something real we might become if conditions are ever right.

- ❖ *Now* is always damp from memory and primed for the guaranteed orgasm of *later*.

- ❖ When the past is kicking at the door, *now* is in the basement calculating the sum of its parts.

- ❖ *Now* loves the space between the first and second horses at the finish.

- ❖ *Now* will collect silently in corners because it's unrecognizable, even to cats.

- ❖ *Now* decays wherever it falls because it has no sense of place.

- ❖ *Now* is exactly when the phone doesn't ring every single time.

## HUMAN VOICES WON'T WORK HERE

He goes in through the mouth, knowing full well it means exiting via the ass. The inside is more complex than a reasonably sized god — a maze of stolen things crushed and toothless in the cage of the individual. The signposts have been pulled up and reoriented; all directions are now one. Guidance must be drawn from only scraps of aging weather. So many steps to master in such tight space will choke the organs. But there is no way back — pressing ahead is the only option. He goes in through the mouth, knowing he may not come out at all. This risk is taken with careful consideration for everyone and no one. He speaks for us all.

## BIVOUAC

Alone by a mountain lake, it is clear — our lives hang on a
thousand tiny filaments in the air. Near dusk, two loons argue
as I boil coffee. Closer to camp, a lonely owl is making speeches
that break and swing in the wind. If I too were a bird, I would
sing my own truth: *distance is a trick of the mind.*

## FOR MY SISTER ON HER 50ᵀᴴ BIRTHDAY

❖ Our old house is no longer a monument to safety. The windows and mirrors quit reflecting truth, and your childhood bedroom ran away.

❖ I hear the rotary phone from the kitchen has been looking for us. It rings sometimes with collect calls from people we forgot to meet.

❖ Much or nothing has changed, depending on your view. Atoms of pure memory reshape themselves and lose value. I split the difference and make do.

❖ The process of becoming still does make a great anthem for the living, but there are some notes only a giant can reach.

❖ When you died, you were wise to hide reminders in the water. You knew the rivers would rise and make strangers of us. Let me be clear: I'm still a soldier for you.

❖ The jaws of the earth, half of an accident, the silent whiff of beyond... Nail these words to the wall wherever it is you sleep. There are no more coming.

## THE REASONS WHY

Because as soon as he was old enough to have a past, he began living there...

Because he made a vow that no one would ever be in position to overthrow him ...

Because he put his faith specifically in those least deserving, just to fuck with them...

Because his mother lived in an igloo made of soda cans and told him chasing joy is hard...

Because he glued his ears shut to block the squeal of time and space...

Because time and space glued their ears shut in response...

Because he kept courting possibility, even though it had already kicked him to the curb...

Because whatever he tried tasted like chicken...

Because what he wanted remained the same despite an influx of new data...

Because the flood of control swept him toward chaos...

Because he was not afraid to admit there was an enormous clock running backward inside him...

Because he knew when to make it stop.

## WHAT THE FUCK

You draw the hours in like cigarette smoke and try to attain the flaming heart of all-at-once — itself a dream borrowed from a death that frames an outcome and forces us to accept (because we already have). Our stay here is described in a pamphlet printed on seawater. It relates a desire to drown each other with words. The story is familiar: Everything is temporary. Divided by delicate walls. Then tomorrow and his brother sneak up and smash your face.

Answer the door, and it's either desire or disease, sprung like a cheetah from the barrel of yesterday, where no one is real but everyone acts like it. Fear of failure is the maternal grandfather of one-quarter of the earth — maybe more. Consider this, or don't. But these days require *presence* — red, green or indifferent. What a pain.

As if enough trouble hadn't found us already, some clown wakes you just to announce that joy will never have fists big enough to defend us. That there will always be goblins chewing at the edge of our peace. That all the stories we wrote are being unwritten every day. But no one can be sure of such things anymore. So much has happened. Go reset the levels on all the controls at the heart of this life.

## THE FUTURE

This place has plans for itself that few can interpret. All that can be seen has an invisible side, too. It's quiet there — an empty spot where the universe should be. It's a whisper of a rock. It's the meaning of fog. It's faith.

There's a coat made of screws in the closet. Remove them one by one and build yourself a tiny future — a time you cannot know. It will take no advice and veer toward the opposite of desire. (This is normal behavior.) Eventually future and already will marry and have three kids with violent, unpronounceable names. Their house will be inside you.

It's OK to move on now. The lessons here were always unlearnable, and reside in a trough of unruly ideas. Too much found and lost. And too much still to come.

## BURIAL AT SEA

Through the starving roof of the world. Into the black of matter. Route and rate of travel are constant. The holes that remain ensure this. Dumb things, blank space without potential, growing ceaselessly. Let enough time go and there is real work on your hands.

No amount of labor can cure the past. Even yesterday. It's not an isolated incident: The whole ocean doesn't listen. What's left is left. Tin sparks in the eyes, floaters that resemble bacteria. Stitch the memories together. Position the plastic animals of thought for a sharper view of it all...

*It's no one's fault.* A statement too often required — how long can we stomach it? Swallow these minerals, liquids, metals. And all our industry that fused them. Wise design and woeful execution. Attention paid or forfeited.

The beginning dissolves in the water of the end. One never knows what to say in these situations. Do you say you're sorry if you weren't there?

## CARNIVAL

We were all supposed to stay together. Some of us didn't get
the message, or chose to ignore it. We did things — fed the
beast or starved it, fell in love, got hurt, healed, fucked and
fought, chose life, changed our minds for a bit, hit peaks and
troughs, flew defiantly into enemy territory only to nosedive
right into love's sad mouth again. We never learned. Or the
things we learned didn't stick. Or were wrong.

There is only enough time to get the things done that we must,
but not any to spare. The things we'd do with extra time are
dreams ripped from a book written by the future and
consumed in fire before we could read it.

There was supposed to be a carnival. There was supposed to
be unbounded joy and an orgy of companionship that blurred
the lines of the self, followed by seemingly endless discussion
and Q&A until the very last question was answered. No one
would be rushed or forgotten. There was supposed to be an
ineffable sense of all life melting together in the sun of a
childhood summer, then carefully wrapped and cooled like ice
cream for a warm afterlife that never comes (and would arrive
with a kind smile if it did).

You should know that out of everyone you were all my favorite,
and we were the best ever, and meant for each other and this

life and its infinite echoes. You should know that you and we and us and them were the only real parts of everything — at least the only parts that everything itself ever cared about and required to be complete. Every tributary and digression in the universe was supposed to live in a single touch we all felt every second.

We were there when the carnival was just opening; we can recall it so clearly. But the rest got stalled and is still stalled. Wrapped up in the red tape of minor disasters happening everywhere at once, with nearly no latency. You think about a moment until time itself disappears and then eventually you know that time will eat anything it reaches. This got screwed up beyond belief because we were all supposed to stay together.

## SAUDADE

I've only now come back to see the old neighborhood is new, so
we really never lived here despite an address to which we
lugged groceries across two boulevards and the park where
old men played pétanque, through an iron door and up four
flights. Despite phone calls and visitors and the cats that slept
at our feet and the ceiling fans that buzzed overhead while we
drank our coffee or whiskey. We never lived here despite this
being the same place where you began to stay over in the
winter and moved in that summer when the city had reignited
itself into a sharp and perfectly disciplined fire like nothing I
could have foreseen, which I recognized on some level but
couldn't name because no other glow was so consuming and
drenched in common joy — through slow sunshine and late
nights with the window open and the feel and taste of your lips
and hips in the dark and the shock of your eyes in the morning
light, eyes that saw everything and nothing in equal measure,
that consumed and digested the hours we inhabited for thirty-
seven months that were the best and only occasionally the
worst but now the ones that have aged just right to live on like
a bright ghost who knows exactly how to tempt me with what I
want so badly and cannot have.

## ANALOGUES

Current circumstances are loud — to cope, we must try to become friends with all the noise. As inhuman features proliferate, you may become a hybrid of everyone you know and a flying spider. This is unsurprising.

The screamers have teeth made of ravens, and soiled fingers where their thoughts should be. They give each new moment a higher price, every fear a unique name; we must be careful not to repeat them. All threats eventually lose some of their evolution, but may claw their way back from most of the typical oblivions.

Best we can do is circle back here and coalesce around a single action: Find the guidepost and burn it to ash. There is no reason to solve the gone days — they are limp and wet with coddling. Better to renovate the possible with pure think-time.

## HOW MEMORY SOUNDS

I have been here the whole time, and this is what I sound like:
Prior things leaking through the eyes, streaming backward on
the wind to the very second this first became now. I am
yesterday, where the present was born, when all the mouths
that spoke for us belonged to others: imagine a clutch of
Romans verbalizing the pulse of a lion to an empty arena. This
isn't real of course. It's just a snapshot of a tumbledown world
designed by those with rough taste. What happens when
existence itself stops and says, "Line, please...?"

Memory is ejected to lighten the load for travel. Memory has no
substance but can kill us all the same. That's a fact. Facts are
how I am now — exactly like you. I wonder if we should split
up to maximize our presence. I wonder if anyone would
notice... or just keep rolling by in the shiny wagons each
creates for the other, spilling truth at every turn until the road
ends in an ocean of free dirt.

## AWAY

We are us. Part of us is not us. On balance, or off — the same is
not different. Our velocity is suspect. We taste doubt in the sky
(it's metallic). What we're now thinking smells rotten because
of goodbye. The ideas we can afford are not constructive. An
end begins because all things are allergic to time. I wish these
boots wouldn't fit anyone. All can be the same if we let it — but
we don't. It's not in our nature to be said, swallowed or unseen.
Sometimes a thing continues without itself.

## EIGHT SENTENCES

❖ Beginnings and ends are simply two different views of the same thing.

❖ The space between a question and an answer has no name — or does it?

❖ I don't know why sometimes we seem to want back what wasn't ever ours.

❖ It takes substance just to understand the realm of the spiritual.

❖ The relationship between life and death is constantly evolving.

❖ I was in the same boat as you right before you drowned — but I got out.

❖ Human beings are quite often present and gone in equal measure.

❖ It's ironic that what you choose to ignore says so much about you.

## ANIMAL

In the mirror, I ask: What is your animal name? Which beast would you follow to reach the end of your argument? I know my answer by a long shot, and will say this: she is a gorgeous calamity. When we understand what to call ourselves, we get one step closer to *home*. Solving for *home* is the equation the gods saddled us with.

It's our job to remember that we are creatures, that all creatures beget struggle, and none are deathproof; nobody is allowed to remain. All life is a wafer of ice on the mind's tongue — wait for it to dissolve then brace for the cold. Those are the only instructions we inherit.

You may feel singular or plural, and each hurts in time. No one really knows where to put their pain. If they claim to, it must belong to someone else. That would be an outright falsehood, just like this: *I once spent the opposite of an hour inside a tiger's mouth.*

## AFFECTION

1.  Where does affection go once it's been trotted out and poked by judges? Liquify it and jar it. Build a stalling mansion of soup behind an icy moat. Some things are best left cold. Most things are best left cold. Fire kills everything two or three times.

2.  I once knew a kid who set fires just to put them out before they did any real damage so he could feel good for doing so. I once knew a kid who used to be mean to animals just to stop before truly hurting them so he could feel good for doing so. They were the same kid, but I liked the fire thing better.

3.  They say you can tell true heroes by the sound of their necks and the color of their ideas. They don't say that. No one says that. *I don't even say that...*

4.  There is so little left to tell. We insult serenity regularly, and sometimes it gets angry. Nothing has infinite patience. You understand nothing in many ways — just not the right one. Nothing has zero tolerance. Deep down we all know the components of zero. Especially the owls.

## POTENTIAL STORY

Someday we will run out of dogs in the fight and everything
will leave itself behind. What happens then is anyone's guess.
Existence, as a story, could cease being written by those who
are here and instead be shaped only by the missing. (This is
troubling.)

We do our best to keep from running aground. We maintain
the course mandated, and try to learn as much as we can.
Surviving thought-winter is the only goal.

So what is the potential story here? The arc of a true hero: One
who rises above all despite low expectations and high odds? Or
the nonhero: One who underwhelms at every turn and kicks
life in the groin for fun? We are all both, and neither. That's the
hard truth. I dare you to tell me different.

## DECISION

Hard to decide what to forget. Days are slippery and often bare.
Like statues. Beyond all that, no one knows which position to
assume later in life — one foreseen, or something cut from
new cloth? It's the little things you imagine and keep secret.
Like horse fingers. It's all the same to strangers, but we are us,
which hurts... Here for a while, then nothing. It's simple to
identify our remains.

Wish there were more to go on. Wish we could keep this
argument as a reminder, but it's bound to decay into soot.
Indulging the past gets pricey. Remember: Only an idea is
permanent. Every tomorrow is the same right now, so take
advantage. Take a breather. Take a good look around, and
you'll see there's slightly less where this came from.

## CONFESSION

Your heart, the sun and a house for regret: The common thread is necessity. Search for something to prove, and hope the effects are felt. Feeling is what we all do. The crucial variable is *self* — the unique fever stamped on your forehead. What do you recognize and promote?

How the days begin and end is the obvious mystery. Salt them all to taste and you'll hardly wonder anything again. Here is the crazy part: Eventually the day comes when all days are counted and evaluated, like employees. A series of metrics is used, but they all miss the mark, knocked off course by a surge of personal fractions.

There are multiple paths to truth. Interrogation is a blunt instrument best saved for endings. Prepare for the questioning all you want, but when the moment comes, you will cave. You'll confess that thinking is a broken luxury. It's what you do to squelch the choice you were born with.

## THESE DAYS

No way to inhabit these days — just sour bones to gnaw. A calendar with a minute hand to mark the time. It's all too close in here, and the air is the wrong size.

Not sure it matters, but complete recall is in the car with us right now. Open the window so he can hang his head out. The tires are flat, but we can pretend to drive.

Remember the befores? Here's one: We raced to the bottom of the lake during an eclipse. The moon saw all of it. I think it was real. But *happened* or *didn't happen* weigh the same at this point. We go nowhere whenever we want.

## TROUBLE'S MOTHER COOKS DINNER

But nobody's hungry. Isn't it always like this? Start winding your way somewhere only to lose the thread in the dark. What a waste of ingredients. *Oh, you're a concrete abstraction. You're a pile of wet hours. You're gone.* These are the things she says.

She says structure is an occasional enemy. It can arrive with a fist or harden slowly like ice. Either way you're captured. There are options, though. So many ways to be done or just beginning. She says take my word for it, even if none of this is accurate.

She says we were once close and caught fire. Fingers pulsed and sought consequence. Now we all wait to rejoin our source. Implement the plan, but remember: Anything visible is only half-written.

## MIRROR IMAGE

We gather at dusk and whisk a finger of bourbon into each dry memory, a recipe for reclaiming time as if prior joy persists, as if it can be gently folded back into *what is*.

Some view the past as an orphaned doll with ashes for hair but others see a living thing — a sugary, naked pang that rises up to embrace us just as all the tiny casualties are brought home. If we could for once solve the argument between *now* and *then*, we'd be golden.

My favorite nowhere twin and I will rest among things *that were* while those *that are* continue stepping around us silently with potential orders from the void: Do not disturb the fragile, swollen depths we plumb for the wisdom of the giant self who dictates the view in every mirror.

## ETERNITY

❖ Eternity was rediscovered. It's sea and sun, fused. It's air-stone. The sum of all things, steeped in boiled time. What is here and gone at once. It will not lose, nor escape loss.

❖ It dissolves in sky, curling morning into blank totems. Who's drawing whistles from the incoming tide? Something was born here already known (like wind). There's a wild seeping. Naked horizon.

❖ Reject the audience assembled by sand kings. Linger among the wet echoes. Set your breath right while eternity sleeps in a nest of music onshore.

❖ See all those things on the *won't rack*: stumble-books, smell of disused spine and fingers, places you will never be from. Lettering is a chore, a silent act of knowledge awaiting reveal.

❖ We get further out every night. The beach always disappears behind swells. Something always touches a leg in the black water. It won't stop. The only way out is through.

❖ Eternity is here again — the drowning stadium, the blind chorus, a pack of instruments murdering a voice. It means less than you think.

## THE END

When the thinking nebulizer kicks in, we all sing the same fog. We can debate whether logic is a decent preservative or if necessity has any other children. But will it lessen the heartbreak of Earth? Which way to move? Which door is lying? Through it all, harm's way is a mood — a choice invented by scorpions. Not the kind you need to achieve apathy.

If we could only taste those mini lifestyles. I want to: plug into narcotic sockets, enjoy a feast of ruined sound, try out the new scream weapon. I want to know about the besides-all-this. The secret with the irregular heartbeat. Then map out a little playroom for Death. Because being right has a very short shelf life.

## SPECTACLE

*I understand. There's an information swarm. If you're unsure, take this one with food...*

There was no foreshadowing the ragged spectacle of us now — something like a three-sided bully threatening a miracle. Most problems are stronger than words. Talk is everywhere, alongside work and death. I could rip out the guts of my thinking and hand it over in a specimen jar, but what tests could we even run?

There's no translation for the ineffable. No way for us to retrace our moves and forge fresh concessions from what lives in the dusk beyond language. So we have only *what is*: 1) A nearly invisible man and woman locked in confusion pulsing from their skin. 2) A collection of illness snapshots taken on a vacation to here. 3) A house that cannot remember its name.

## NOTE TO YOU ABOUT THE BEYOND

This is an alarm... this is a test... this is a special germ. Goes from one body to another on whispered paws. I am trying to tell you there is still *the beyond*, and it is closer now. This much is obvious even without measurement... I was you once. And again. And always. But what I love about *you+me* the most burns brighter now. Reminds me of everything there ever was and could be. Of nothing... It's a zero-consumption game — all things go back to where they were in the end. We can win without playing. Don't even start. I promise not to end... That is how it goes: We see within us what we are missing, what we threw away but claim was stolen. We are together especially when apart. We are the screech of a troubled animal in a cloud at the beginning of the planet... If we were a drug, I would take far more than recommended. That is all I'm saying.

## THE OCEAN PHONE

At the end of the end past the soul's eye, there is a negative lamp — one that spreads darkness in its immediate vicinity. Let this thought into the world and it could punch holes in every imaginable surface, with murk rising to create desperate new islands. We could give these islands names like Speculation, Outrage, Wonder. Does an island carry itself differently once it has something to be called? Is it less isolated?

*** 

We behave like photons, bursting a short distance before absorption by hungry molecules. We share a set of basic properties: Nothingness awaits us. We are commercially impractical, but emotionally viable. We add cost and complexity to any process. We cannot authenticate each other in advance. We cannot trust the medium between all things. Anxiety is a common code. We become mostly massless, with expansive impacts.

***

Consider these words purposeful distractions. Here's what is important: Right now there is an abundance of purpose. Right now there is activity kidnapping progress. Right now there are people in the gathering dusk, lined up to beg favors from their history on the ocean phone.

***

In this place, you can only count backwards — from zero to small zero. This is a broken scene stolen by the hive and stashed in a nearby throat. The walls drip open secrets.

Someone told us language is a sin, so we stopped even thinking. Someone else said sins aren't real, but we forgot who it was. One thing is true: Only the purest rivers of sorrow feed their own source. The delta where we lived is flooded with apologies. Underneath it's a mess of flesh and geometry. Who can translate?

Or maybe just ignore all this before it's finished. Before anything starts again. Before nothing intrudes. Right now clock hands trace the calf of a woman made of past. Time to go.

## LION

Yes, there will always be a temptation to shoot off eight
tongues' worth of longing before the bus even makes its first
stop and we have yet to see which one of the coming hot-
shifting delights has the most cream or least acid — a time
when no one should be making thoughts or nonthoughts or
any mind action, lest we tip the balance too far toward the
central mess without asking the right permissions — and given
the lack of concretion at this stage of the ride, it would make
sense to assume a place in both front and back to cover every
angle, not missing a shard of potential and thus not being
whipped and stabbed by regret because you didn't allow
yourself (or even a suitable proxy) to locate the only true
fireplace and let the correct flame grow and sprawl
respectfully within the vast-glorious heart of the lion.

## OBSERVATIONS FROM THE ATTIC OF SUMMER'S ABANDONED HOUSE

1. Condensed ideas distort a glass landscape. Heat drives motion in time. The vibrational churn of words. The birth of discrete hurt particles again. The rising many-body predicate. All part of an elegant problem to admire.

2. Life is a car fueled by malice. It collides with things to make them whole. Life begins at foreplay and ends at birth. Life begins at birth and ends at a party for hungry ghosts. Life begins in moisture and doesn't end.

3. What happens next is the trick. (We've heard it before: "Next is all we have in the end. And the beginning. Next is all there ever was. Managing next is the only real job on earth.") Ownership of next is still unresolved, so we catch up on sleep.

4. We are all electric meat — small, derelict things. We can begin the self-reorganization process anytime now, but always opt not to. We can finally steal safety from the tired jaws of the wolf, but instead feed him our friends. Mostly we just automate the

output and set the dial to half-equilibrium, half-terror.

5. We counter bursts of wet red force with localized micro-faiths; it comes to nothing. It's an object lesson in failure scrawled in the margins of a high school textbook... Just like the teacher told us, "There's no reconciling decaying licks of flame. But good luck."

6. I have a pattern in my head of a sunflower. I have electromagnetic traps in my mouth. I have virtually no velocity left. But I want. And I am waiting. I have been waiting since everyone's first birthday. When do the winners get the prize? When do the losers know they've lost? *Why so long?*

Made in the USA
Columbia, SC
01 February 2025